Abundance in the Thunder

Stacey Aromando

ISBN 978-1-68570-551-0 (paperback)
ISBN 978-1-68570-552-7 (digital)

Christian Faith Publishing
832 Park Avenue
Meadville, PA 16335
www.christianfaithpublishing.com

Printed in the United States of America

Preface

To encourage
To elevate
To motivate
To never underestimate
To have the power within your abdundant thunder

Introduction

This book is meant to inspire those who lost, who feel lost, and who still believe. The book was written as if I were looking at life through another person's eyes or his or her experiences.

A special thank you to my parents and extended family, Hailey Marie and Derek Jordan, Cynthia and Family, Anthony, and everyone from Milton Ave, Joann Morina, CLL, Christine Lilore, Diane Riker, the Delbarton Family, Joey Panzitta, Nikki, Ashley, Vonette, David M. Kaufman, MD, William R. Chenitz, MD, Swami Nathan, MD, Jared Sullivan, MD, and staff, Sylvia Coscia, MD, Margaret Blackwood, MD, and Marilyn and John Carlin, Jill Preis. I'd also like to include all my new friends from Kings Bedminster and Nutley, New Jersey.

I am grateful to the people who donated to my Go Fund Me page to start me off with this project: Naika Fleuristal, Louis Ross, Reverend Mark Thompson, Kelly Rotondo, Jennifer Armstrong, Kaliah Smith, Jardley Sosa, and Ebony Atwell. I'm eternally grateful to Nadia Comaneci, Eric Heiden, Joel Osteen Ministries, Mickaila Sands, the Donoghue and McCarthy families, and the Catholic charities and churches around the world.

Stacey has been reached in many ways and entertained by T. D. Jakes, Tyler Perry, Artie Lange, Robert Deniro, Al Pacino, Chris Rock, Wendy Williams, Black Uhuru, Bob Marley and The Wailers, Jimmy Buffet, Dennis Brown, Howard, Robin, and Gary, Queen Latifah, Kevin James, Sebastian Maniscalco, and Mike Marino (comedian).

The Questions We Are Afraid to Ask

MAY 30, 2013

What would Jesus do if he saw you crying in the rain?
What would Jesus do if he saw you all torn up?
What would Jesus do if he saw you driving on the road?
What would he do in your last hour?

What would Jesus do if he saw you living in poverty?
Would he grab hold of your hand or just decide to walk you along the way?

What would Jesus do if you were told you had three hours to live?
Would he bless you with prayers and take away all your sadness?

The truth is that Jesus doesn't have to be asked what he would do and neither do we
He does every minute, every hour, and every year.
He blesses, he prays, he brings us to our greatness.

Surviving

JULY 18, 2020

Tough streets
Tough minds
Mean street creeps
Tough minds

We all reach
We all try
Tough minds
We continue to cry

Tough life
Mean streets
Tough minds
We all seek to find

We hold on
We hold out
Tough minds
We are strong
No doubt

In The Wake Of The Haiti Earthquake

AUGUST 29, 2011

They said their eyes were watching God
They didn't worry about the sun rolling through the clouds
They never imagined the heat and the desperation
They never knew that they were part of a bigger situation

The poorer the country, the poorer the people
The silent angel voices screaming from out of the steeple
The morning dew blanketed their worlds and
The nighttime fires would make their hair curl
The aid was sent from around the world, and the doctors flew quickly to
help and console
The people accepted the food, but it was removed swiftly

They couldn't hold on to the hope and faith
They couldn't believe that they were on the right path
Suddenly the gods and angels held out their hand, and the reality is the
larger and indefinite plan

We stretch out our hearts across the land
We only hope that the rest of the world will understand

Dedication To Life's Strongest

JULY 12, 2003

Boston Strong, We don't know what went wrong
A special anniversary, 35th running strong
The gun went off, the runners began
The crowds gathered, the course was planned

It was a usual April day
Patriots and runners came to pray
The ritualistic 26.2 miles so far, so strong
Boston strong, we don't know what went wrong

It's upsetting to know a bomb was planned
To harm, to hurt, to destroy and to descend
The supportive crowds filled with moms and dads
Children and extended family all were there and were glad

The smoke appeared, the sun set in
The madness developed, and some runners life's would end
Two master minded young men decided to mame
The runners and their families would never be the same

Boston strong, the days are long
Boston strong, we cannot go wrong
We are Boston strong across the globe
Wake up America, stop acting like you don't know

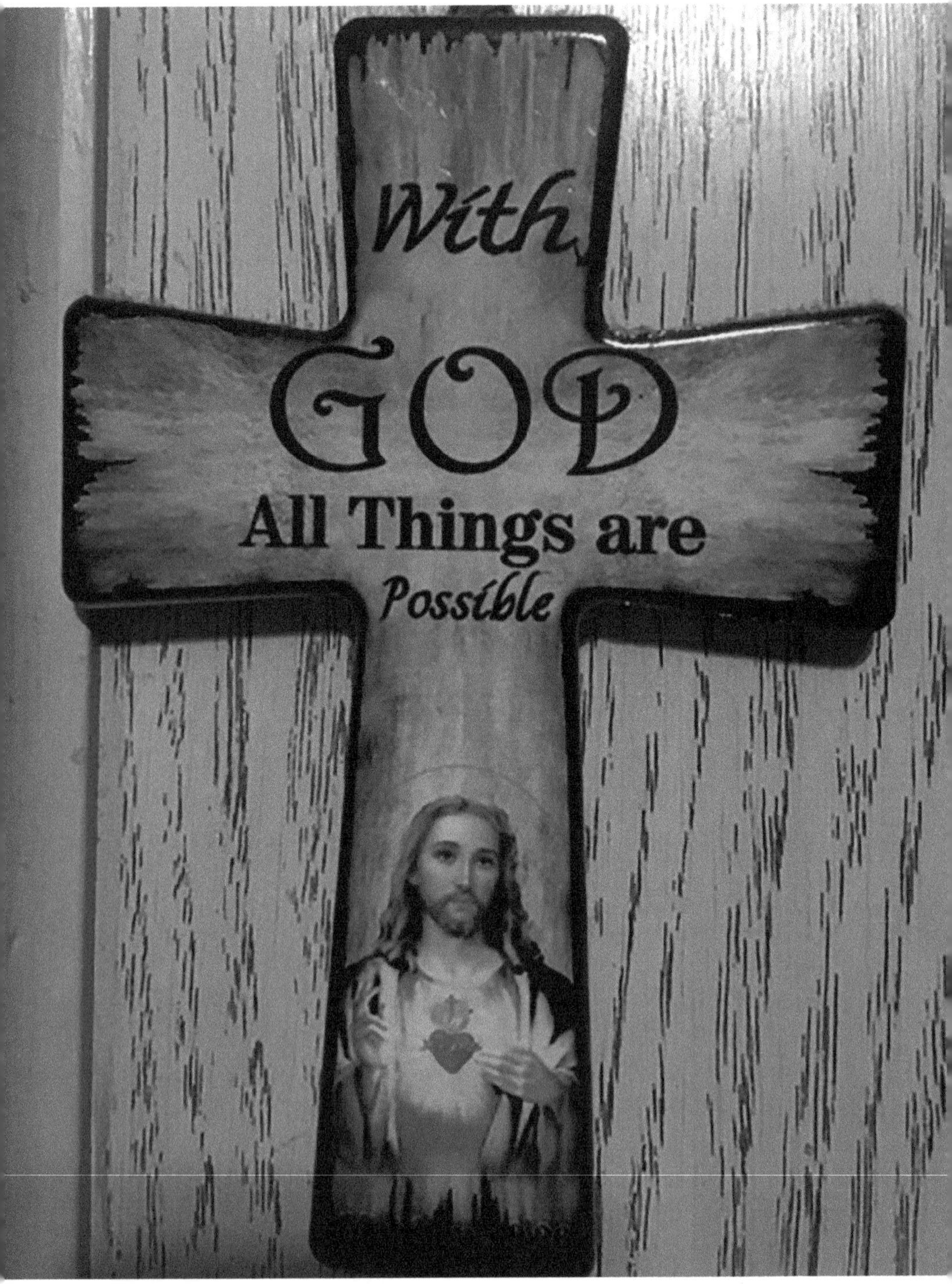
With
GOD
All Things are
Possible

Give It to God

AUGUST 30, 2021

Give it to God when your heart is uncertain
Give it outwardly and not behind the curtain
Give it to God
The Lord helps all
Give it to God
We have to fall
Give it to God
He makes us great
Give it to God
It's never too late

A Reach

MAY 16, 2021

Reach out for the Lord
Sing him praise, and kneel down today
Reach out for the Lord
Shout his name out; let him pray
Reach out for the Lord
Show him you mean it
Let him know you can achieve even if it's only a little bit

Reach out for the Lord
It's the meaning of your soul
It's the way of the Lord to make you whole
Without our Lord, it would be a darker tomorrow
A day without hope and a feeling of more sorrow

Reach out for the Lord
He redeems us and makes us so much better
It's time now to reach for the stars and allow the Lord to bless you with
his faithful letter

Angels On The Windowsill

AUGUST 15, 2011

There are angels on your windowsill every day of your life
They float within the sunbeams and wipe out all your strife
They seep into your pores in the very early morning dew
You would be surprised how many are watching you when you're feeling
blue

There are angels on your windowsills on crisp autumn mornings
You know, early November at 5:00 a.m., just when you get up and are
still yawning
Reach out your hand, and say a prayer of faith
Because you never know when it's your time to meet at heaven's gate

There are angels on your windowsill when the snow is falling late
The winter nights at 5:00 p.m., the ones that make our hearts race
You never have to worry about the angels running away
Appreciate their presence when loved ones are led astray

I cannot begin to express the angels who remain
The ones who live through others and are actually the same
If you see an angel sitting on your windowsill today
Realize the gift of love and faith and how they teach us how to continue
to pray

We Reign

JULY 18, 2020

We reign through smoke
We reign through hate
We reign through misery
We reign through history

We reign when we are told we cannot
We reign because we are heaven-sent
We reign through terror
We reign and never say never

We keep it real
We reign and feel
We reign when we heal
We are always told that we steal

No one can stop our reign
We climb a mountain and conquer it whole
We were always told we were callous and cold
The love in our hearts will reign on strong
You're never so true when they find out they are wrong

Keep up your reign
Wherever you may be
Keep up your reign, and let the whole world see

Bullets In My Brain

JULY 18, 2020

A bullet hit me in my brain
A bullet made me totally insane
A bullet hit me in my heart
A bullet tore us far apart

A bullet made both of us stand out
A bullet hit my inner soul
A bullet made their heads roll
A bullet hit the center of my eye
A bullet gave me every reason to try
A bullet lit a fire
A bullet made them a liar

No justice, no life
Bullets bring sorrow
Bullets are not a better tomorrow

To Wear A Crown

MAY 27, 2009

I wear the crown; you are a saint
I wear the crown; you seem distant
You gave the glory; I received the prize
I wear the crown even though you lied

The possessions of the crown are filled with the jewels
You gave a prize that kept me from losing

To give glory is to get glory
To see the glory is to know the story
You were glorified the day you were baptized
You were rectified the day the Lord was sanctified
To remember the glory days is to remember how to survive the purple haze
The remaining part of this glory note goes,

For those who want the glory
You need to understand the entire story
To want the glory
Know the story
To want the glory
Believe the story

Glorify
Sanctify
You earned the glory

The Diary Of A Fallen Star

SEPTEMBER 25, 2011

I wiped my tears a thousand times
I watched America suffer countless crimes
I reached for hope, and you held my hand
We talked about the reasons and how to understand

You commanded the angels, and they danced through my soul
We worked through the tough times and reached for the gold
We wore the crown, and held our head up so boldly
We kept our direction and mindset; yes, we held on strongly

Tick, tick, the clock kept running
Tick, tick, we would not stop winning
It was time to slow it down
It was time to run fast
It was always time to set the record straight and make the memories last

We reign because we worked hard
We reign because we were told it was never ours
You cannot take away the races won and miles we ran
We stand so proudly because we always believed we can

Did You Burn Your Bridges?

SEPTEMBER 25, 2011

Did you cross the bridge to seek for hope?
A better life and a brand-new way to cope
Did you cross the bridge to end your sins?
Deep in the oceans, where the wave spins
Did you see the bridge crash to the ground under the stars with no one around?
Did you look for bridges to separate your life?
A bridge of peace and no more strife,
The bridge of equality of strength and faith,
A bridge of prayer, one that can keep you in good health!

Strangers To The Crown

MAY 27, 2009

Sitting strong on the throne enough to feel proud
Sitting alone on the throne wrapped in nails and chains, you wear the crown
Realizing today that nothing is ever going to be the same
You're sitting on the throne, awaiting to be praised
There is never a moment that the throne has to be raised
Since the blood from the nails of the crown continue to be around
It continues to encourage the people who were lost then found

Blessings For The King of Pop

OCTOBER 19, 2011

I'm hurting Lord, I'm in pain
I'm crying Lord, can you see the rain
I'm filled with tears, my life is gone
I'm hurting Lord, I wonder what went wrong

It's been a lonely life, a year of blues
It's been a lonely day, a year of mistakes
I know you hear me Lord, we talk each day
I never really got to tell you everything I wanted to say
The pain is daily, my body is weak
My years of fame are for others to speak

The crowds are gone, the cheers are low
I never wanted to end the daily flow
I screamed at night, my body was decaying
I never worried what others were saying
I told my secrets and shared my joys
I closed my eyes to shut out the noise

Is It Worth It?

JANUARY 7, 2014

Don't let anyone determine your worth
I've been like this from the day of my birth
If you have black diamonds in your heart
You have to swallow white pearls two days apart

Don't let anyone determine your worth
It's not a dime
It's not a quarter
It's not a dollar
It's only your higher power that determines your worth

The Two-And-A-Half-Year Plan

AUGUST 8, 2014

They say I have two and half years
Time to laugh and time for tears
A time to reflect and celebrate life
To enjoy the rest of the ride
And forget the strife
A breath of fresh air on a September day
A nighttime cap in October, July, or May
A simple walk and a long, hard run
Time with my children to laugh and have fun
Reaching out to my family and friends
Remembering all the good times we had
Teaching others what I learned in the past
Warning young girls not to grow up too fast

A Million Dollars

OCTOBER 5, 2019

If you won a million dollars, would you give it to the Lord?
Would you bring it to the ocean and watch the seagulls soar?
If you won a million dollars, would you sell your soul for gold?
Would you leave your home and family and start a whole new world?

If you won a million dollars and lived your life over,
would you thank God for everything and watch him take over?
Would you take your million dollars and take it to an altar?
Or would you thank Jesus for helping you and try to live better?

A Wall For Whitney

MY SHOOP GIRL

FEBRUARY 15, 2012

You grew up a model, a star, and a leaf in the wind
You never knew the pressure that you would face in the end
Your family encouraged every move that you made
Your singing brought you stardom, and you made the grade

The streets of New Jersey were always your home
The world applauded your voice and your songs
You sold millions, and your fans were thrilled
Record upon record, and Clive footed the bill
To learn that demons took your spirit away
Is the underestimate of your last day

You thanked your Jesus and Robyn daily and held them
In your heart
Precious friends and family surrounded you and wanted to believe it
It was a farce
It's silent now, and the choir still sings with you there
It's that beautiful image of your smile and your stare

The Oil Is Bleeding

JANUARY 18, 1991

The war has begun, and the raindrops turned into sun
The soldiers are proud that their country is one
The people at home are hostile because they want peace
The enemy country is determined to not cease
The guns and the planes are circling the sky
Never to stop but only to die

The young men who wake up at dawn
Pray every night that they will soon be at home
The children in the schools are scared and alone
The family is separate and destroyed to the bone
We must not forget the times that we live
In historical society, it's taking and giving
Those who feel that their day is bad
Should remember the boys who are strong and proud
The president sent them to a country with unrest
And many of the boys will be remembered as the country's best

Honors Of Love

FEBRUARY 21, 2010

To gain a crown
To see the smile
To gain a power
The thought of knowledge

To gain the kingdom
We bow down to pray
To gain the honors
We know what to say

We take it slow
We see our life
We follow order
If we do not, we live in strife

To gain the jewels, we know the flight
You get the crown and reach for it with all your might
To gain the courage and feel encouraged
You cannot lose, do not feel discouraged

Tragedy In The Blue

JUNE 15, 2020

Our arms are with Jesus
Our hands are held up
Our arms are with the people
We will not be told to shut up

Our arms are with Jesus
We will not be held down
Our message is one thing
We are not white; we are not brown

Our arms are with Jesus
We pray this daily hymn
Our hands are held high
In the future we will win

Don't let Jesus down
Don't let us down either
Don't let Jesus down
Let us breathe a little easier

My Tears
APRIL 9, 2020

My tears are falling because you are gone
My tears are falling because they thought it was wrong
My tears are falling because we sang that song
My tears are falling because it's been so long

Wipe your tears away, and let them fall
Wipe your tears away, and don't answer the call
Wipe your tears away, and let them fall
Wipe your tears away, and keep standing tall

Teardrops disappear inside my mind and heart
Teardrops look away from that broken heart
You were my teardrop, and you are my past
You were my heartache, and you're not my last

To Understand I Am

I am the dream
I am what it seems
I am in control
I dream the good fight
I am as good as dynamite

I want the best and not to fail
I am what I am and told to prevail
I am too much and sometimes not enough
I am so sweet, and always I am tough enough
I am in control of loving you
I am in control of providing for you

I am the one in control
I am in control of being there for you
I am in control and believe I can make millions
I am in control of everything

Do You Believe

1-17-2020

Christ failed us?
Christ protect us?
Christ help us to cope
Help us hang on to hope
Help us not to give up

Our hearts have drowned
Our hearts are thrown around
We are what we are and what we allow
Christ we love you and you deserve a bow

We do not understand why you saved some and not all
We realize tomorrow is not promised and we all have to fall
We grow when we fail and we grow when we succeed
We know that Christ is there for us to allow us to see

It is in the thunder when we are scared the most
In our darkest moments is when we grow to our very best
Christ believes in us and we must pay it forward
Christ does not let us down even when we ignore him

Moonbeams For Jay-Z
From A Fan

SEPTEMBER 23, 2013

Meltdown showdown showtime
Silver and gold bars
Walk the pathways of underground, a pathway to the stars
You prospered, we grew, you feel, and I knew
The spotlight shines on those who pray
The spotlight brings those together who went astray
Never gave up, my time is just beginning
It's Jay, and it's embracing resilience, and you come up winning

Your mic is covered with diamonds and pearls
Your fame and fortune are as strong as your golden girls
It is a new day, and the show must go on
It's time for the audience to listen to the song

Christmas In Heaven

NOVEMBER 2, 2014

It is Christmas in heaven
The angels are lined up to total the number of seven
It is Christmas in heaven in the midst of the clouds
The angels are dancing and shouting out loud

The Christmas songs are playing in heaven
The angels are there to make sure it is even
It is Christmas in Jersey; it is purely heaven
The Christmas cheers are beginning
It is Christmas in heaven; we gather around to love and hug
It is Christmas in heaven; someone is watching from up above

Heaven knows; heaven glows
Heaven is seven angels; heaven glows
The seven stars, the tireless angels of heaven
The simple breath of love from heaven

A Marines Life-Semper Fi

OCTOBER 30, 2021

First one in and last one out
First one in and no one shouts
First one in and we cheer them on
First one in and last one done

Semper Fi, we honor the best
Semper Fi, we expect nothing less
Trained in the heat and in the rain
Some of the boys will never be the same

Through World War 1 and World War 2
The Vietnam War and Desert Storm too
There is never a complaint or why or how come
Marines get it done under the clouds and sun

Strange things have been said about our green berets
Why on earth would people think a flag couldn't be waved
Marine life and service life is all some know
Whether it is a volunteer, a purple heart or a drafted boy

The message is: Got it done and they deserve praise

Through mountains and jungles and fields and streams
Sometimes their life's were never what it seemed
Locked and loaded through thick and thin
How these boys are sometimes not honored is a living sin

While judgement can only be passed by the man above
The signs of courage are the eagle and the dove
Keeping their faith while days were so dark
Honoring the United States is always a must

If Michael Could Sing

FEBRUARY 2010

A song of hope,
a song of praise
Michael lived for everlasting praise
He sings for glory and self-determination, and his words were silent, and
he fought for admiration
The longer he sang, the more he danced
We remember him today by a shadow of a glance

Nine O'clock Always A Prince

FEBRUARY 2010

They call him the Prince of Peace
The King of kings
We call him the Prince of Peace
The leader of all rings

The peace he gives
The peace we live
The peace he sings
The peace we live

They call him the Prince of Peace
He died on the cross
We call him the Prince of Peace
And all our sins he tossed

They call him the Prince of Peace
He made that sacrifice
We call him the Prince of Peace
And anything he does will suffice

The peace he gives
The peace he leaves
The peace he breathes
The Prince of Peace he is

Hope

FEBRUARY 2010

Having
Outstanding
Perseverance
Everlasting

If Angels Could Talk

SEPTEMBER 10, 2011

They call it ground zero, three thousand or more gone
We call it New York City, one million or more strong
By the grace of God, some of us survived
By the grace of God, the fires turned into cries
The angels could talk while saving those who jumped
The reason this happened has left America stunned

They say we all had wings and we wanted the smoke to clear
We always looked further so that our angel wings could soar
The hurt, the loss, the sound of the buildings crumbling
The smoke got in our eyes
The courageous policemen and the firemen were the angels in disguise

Don't let your hearts be troubled, and believe that life was good
God watched over us that day and knew that saving their souls was
understood
It doesn't take the pain away or the people who passed
It restored the souls of survivors and left their hearts stacked

The Mystery Of Love

APRIL 6, 2012

The stations of the cross, a time of impending sorrow
The memories of yesterday in good times, so borrowed
We asked our Lord for forgiveness, and he did the same
The crowds of people applauded him and cried when he was maimed
The days of our lives and the chains we carry daily
The sins that haunt us in our darkest hour, he offered his love so freely
It is your cross to bear, the day you want it to end
See it as forgiveness, not fear, just a way to transcend

Shining Angel

FEBRUARY 11, 2009

Shining angel, shine down on my heart
Realize today your life was set apart
Shining angel, stay strong and breathe
Show your strength, fight the good fight, feel relieved

See, justice will be served
Justice will be a long time coming
Shine down on our fallen angel
The hurt will be no longer

To Save A Life

APRIL 25, 2020

I was called to serve you and save your life
I was called to save you and make your world bright
I was called to serve you and help you breathe
I was called to serve you and keep you relieved

You have never met me, and today we became friends
I was called to serve you until the bitter end
You called for help, and I jumped right in
l tried to relieve your struggling grin
I served you today, and we left total strangers
I wonder if tomorrow, when I serve you, if you got any better

In The Presence Of Angels

AUGUST 8, 2008

12 angels standing in a line
12 angels holding on to time
12 angels shouting at the devil
12 angels hoping the sentence is better

If you see twelve angels and are praying for good
Never say "I wished that I should"
12 angels are present at the beginning of your day
12 angels have more than a little something to say

12 angels are guarding your soul
12 angels don't want you to pay this toll
Ask the angels to forgive you today
And you will be surprised at your sentence, what they have to say

Forgive

JANUARY 3, 2021

Forgive the person who hurt you the most
Forgive those who tried to take away your thirst
Forgive those who tried to steal your joy
Forgive those who told you that you couldn't be much more

Forgive those who purposely tried to hurt you
Forgive those who told you to forget your virtues
Forgive those who didn't bother to walk beside you
Forgive those who, when you were happy, tried to make you feel blue
Forgive those and forgive yourself
Forgive the world, and let Jesus take over the rest

Glorified
FEBRUARY 2, 2014

Glorified and sanctified forever, we survived
Glorified and sanctified forever, we will try

Try to overcome
Try to hide the fear
Try to overcome
Try to see through the tears

Glorified and sanctified
Forever we survive
Try to share a smile
Try to go that extra mile
Inside our heads, we knew we would try
Inside our hearts, we knew it was a lie

Don't give up hope
Don't think of it as a struggle

We Will Never Forget

SEPTEMBER 10, 2011

We will never forget; we stand by our flag
Our towers were crumbled, and our hearts continue to drag
We will stand by the ghosts of the towers that were there
The thousands of people who died on 9/11 will always be there

It's a cemetery but a galaxy of stars
Families of angels looking through the steel bars
The cross remains frozen; the ashes never left
The souls of the victims transpired into dust

It's ten years past, ten years too long
We continue to see our firefighting brothers and sing that song
We will never forget; we still stand strong
Dear Lord, what on earth did America do wrong?

A Word Of Hope To All
The Single Mommies

JANUARY 1, 1995

I hope for you a better day
I hope your life will be treasured with hurrays
I hope your dreams will all come true
I hope through difficult times you will believe the Lord will see you through
I hope your words will always be kind
I hope, the day you give birth, your sorrows will be left behind

Stay strong and blessed
Never give up
If you believe your blessed
You can always achieve

About The Author

Stacey is a gifted writer and life coach who has inspired many on a personal and professional level. She starts her day daily by giving praise to the Almighty and focusing on paying it forward. She is blessed with a gift of encouraging words for all whom she meets and has worked in the medical field for over thirty-five years with an interest in patient care and veterinarian medicine with ten years of experience working for veterinarians in the past. Her passion at this point in her life is Namaste yoga, traveling, attending Broadway and comedy shows. Stacey enjoys listening to a wide variety of music. B. B. King, Billie Holiday, Louis Armstrong, Neil Young and Crazy Horse, The Beatles, Rolling Stones, Alicia Keys, Prince, Rhianna, Mariah, Alt Nation, 92.3 K-Rock, Lorde, Stevie Ray Vaughan, Channel 39 Hair Nation, and CCR are just a few of many musicians that she admires. She resides twelve miles outside Manhattan and enjoys her love for animals and volunteer experiences in the past for Veteran Affairs, local home bound neighbors, and suicide intervention programs. Her fondest memories are from the 1970s and 1980s with her participation in long distance road racing, with the likes of the late Tom Fleming, Grete Waitz, Joan Benoit, Patti Catalano, Bill Rodgers, Martha White, Nancy Seeger, Doreen Ennis Schwartz, Miki Gorman, and many other star athletes. This book is part of a series totaling four.

CPSIA information can be obtained
at www.ICGtesting.com
Printed in the USA
BVHW022148240622
640658BV00014B/208

9 781685 705510